2.0

Australian Animals
Platypuses

By Sara Louise Kras

Consulting Editor: Gail Saunders-Smith, PhD

Content Consultant: Bob Cleaver, owner
Wombat Rise Sanctuary, a home for rescued Australian wildlife
Sandleton, South Australia

Capstone
press®

Mankato, Minnesota

Pebble Plus is published by Capstone Press,
151 Good Counsel Drive, P.O. Box 669, Mankato, Minnesota 56002.
www.capstonepub.com

072010
005866R

 Books published by Capstone Press are manufactured with paper
containing at least 10 percent post-consumer waste.

Library of Congress Cataloging-in-Publication Data
Kras, Sara Louise.
  Platypuses / by Sara Louise Kras.
    p. cm. — (Pebble plus. Australian animals)
  Includes bibliographical references and index.
  Summary: "Simple text and photographs present platypuses, how they look,
where they live, and what they do" — Provided by publisher.
  ISBN 978-1-4296-3312-3 (library binding)
  ISBN 978-1-4296-3870-8 (pbk.)
  1. Platypus — Juvenile literature. I. Title. II. Series.
QL737.M72K73 2010
599.2'9 — dc22   2008051182

Editorial Credits
Jenny Marks, editor; Bobbie Nuytten and Ted Williams, designers; Svetlana Zhurkin, media researcher

Photo Credits
Alamy/Gerry Pearce, cover
Getty Images/National Geographic/Jason Edwards, 21
Minden Pictures/D. Parer & E. Parer-Cook, 5, 15; Reg Morrison, 13
Peter Arnold/BIOS/Dave Watts, 7, 9; Biosphoto/J.-L. Klein & M.-L. Hubert, 19; Gunter Ziesler, 11; TUNS, 17
Shutterstock/Del Bauchat Grant, 1

Note to Parents and Teachers

The Australian Animals set supports national science standards related to life science. This
book describes and illustrates platypuses. The images support early readers in understanding
the text. The repetition of words and phrases helps early readers learn new words. This book
also introduces early readers to subject-specific vocabulary words, which are defined in the
Glossary section. Early readers may need assistance to read some words and to use the Table of
Contents, Glossary, Read More, Internet Sites, and Index sections of the book.

Table of Contents

Living in Australia

A very unusual animal
lives in Australia.
This furry creature
is called a platypus.

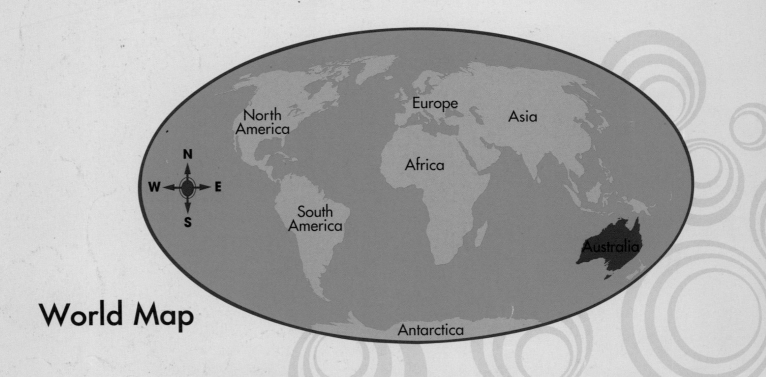

World Map

North America

Europe

Asia

Africa

South America

Australia

Antarctica

N

W E

S

Platypuses live near streams
and ponds in Australia.
They slide from their burrows
into the water.

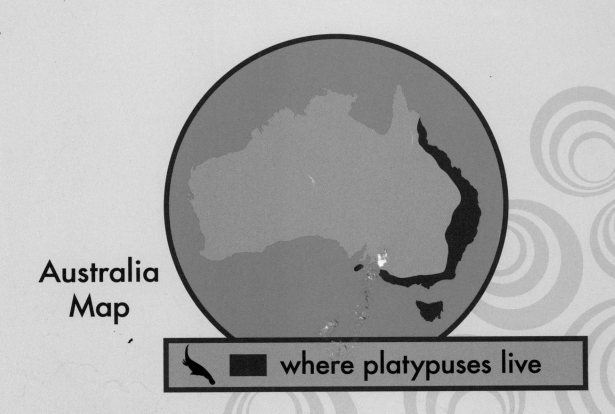

Australia
Map

where platypuses live

Up Close!

Platypuses can grow 20 inches
(51 centimeters) long.
Males weigh up to 4 pounds
(1.8 kilograms).
Females are smaller.

6

Platypuses are good swimmers
and divers.
Their webbed feet
and round, flat tails
push them through the water.

A platypus sometimes swims

in icy water.

Two thick coats of fur

keep its body warm and dry.

Finding Food

A platypus cannot see
or hear well in the water.
Its soft bill uses
electroreceptors to find food.

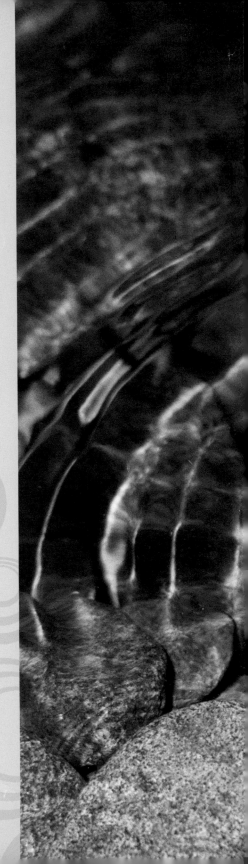

Platypuses eat eggs, tiny bugs,
worms, and shellfish.
Platypuses do not have teeth.
They grind gravel in their mouths
to break down their food.

Life Cycle

The platypus is one

of two mammals that lay eggs.

A platypus lays her eggs

deep in a burrow.

Her body keeps them warm.

When young platypuses hatch,
they are blind and hairless.
They stay safe in the burrow.
In four months, they will be
ready to swim in the pond.

Glossary

bill — a ducklike beak; platypuses have wide, soft bills.

burrow — a tunnel or hole in the ground made or used by an animal

electroreceptor — one of many small cells that sense the electricity in other animals

hatch — to break out of an egg

mammal — a warm-blooded animal that has a backbone and hair or fur; female mammals feed milk to their young.

shellfish — an underwater creature with a hard outer shell

webbed — connected by a fold of skin; platypuses have webbed toes.

Read More

Arnold, Caroline. *A Platypus' World*. Caroline Arnold's Animals. Mankato, Minn.: Picture Window Books, 2008.

Caper William. *Platypus: A Century-Long Mystery*. Uncommon Animals. New York: Bearport, 2009.

Collard, Sneed B. *A Platypus, Probably*. Watertown, Mass.: Charlesbridge, 2005.

Internet Sites

FactHound offers a safe, fun way to find Internet sites related to this book. All of the sites on FactHound have been researched by our staff.

Here's all you do:

Visit *www.facthound.com*

FactHound will fetch the best sites for you!

Index

Word Count: 178

Grade: 1

Early-Intervention Level: 24